AF615472

CHILDREN OF HONG KONG

Children In A Changing World

CHILDREN OF HONG KONG

By Terry Shannon

Illustrated with photographs

Maps and drawings by Charles Payzant

A GOLDEN GATE JUNIOR BOOK   CHILDRENS PRESS • CHICAGO

Shannon, Terry.
Children of Hong Kong.

(Children in a changing world)
"A Golden Gate junior book."
Includes index.
SUMMARY: Simple text and illustrations introduce the home, family, and daily activities of several children living in Hong Kong.
1. Children in Hongkong—Juvenile literature.
[1. Children in Hongkong. 2. Hongkong—Social life and customs] I. Payzant, Charles, ill. II. Title.
HQ792.H6S47 301.43'14'095125 74-23790
ISBN 0-516-08885-8

Manufactured in the United States of America
Designed by Charles Payzant

1 2 3 4 5 6 7 8 9 10 11 12 13 14 15 R 81 80 79 78 77 76 75

ACKNOWLEDGEMENTS

For their generous cooperation in my search for background material and for photographs made available for use in this book, material which has added greatly to the on-the-spot information which I gleaned and to the photographs taken by me, the author's sincere appreciation goes to the Hong Kong Government Information Services, especially to Mr. Grahame S. Blundell, M.B.E., and Mr. George Yuen of that office; and to the Hong Kong Tourist Association.

I also wish to express my thanks to Mr. C. Y. Tung, Head of the C. Y. Tung Group (Island Navigation Corp., etc.), and Captain John Tuanmu of that company's Hong Kong office, for their hospitality and several kindnesses to me while I was in Hong Kong.

Among others who were helpful (many whose names I do not know), I wish to thank Mr. Peter Ching for his hospitality at yum char, his family and Kowloon shop served as inspiration for a portion of this book.

And last, but by no means least, I wish to dedicate this book to my associate, Charles Payzant, the artist half of the author-artist team known as Shannon-Payzant, and to acknowledge his unstinting efforts in many behind-the-scenes activities such as designing this and our many preceding books, the earlier ones illustrated with his fine artwork.

Nearly half of all the people who live in teeming Hong Kong are girls and boys under the age of sixteen. Among them are children with names such as Li Po, Jade Wu, and Ding Chau, and their lives differ somewhat from one another.

Just as elsewhere, the fathers and mothers of Hong Kong children have various ways of earning a living. This affects where and how families live and where children go to school. So, if you were a Chinese child living in Hong Kong, a girl named Wong Pei might be your schoolmate. Perhaps a boy named Peter Ling might be your neighbor. Or an English girl named Sarah Jordan might be your friend. These are children you'll read about in this book.

But before we meet children of Hong Kong with their various life styles, let's find out a bit about this place that fascinates people the world over, this place of many children.

Hong Kong is a British Crown Colony, just as certain parts of the United States were once British colonies. It lies thousands of miles across the Pacific Ocean from North America. It is one of our more distant neighbors. It is also thousands of miles from Great Britain to which it belongs.

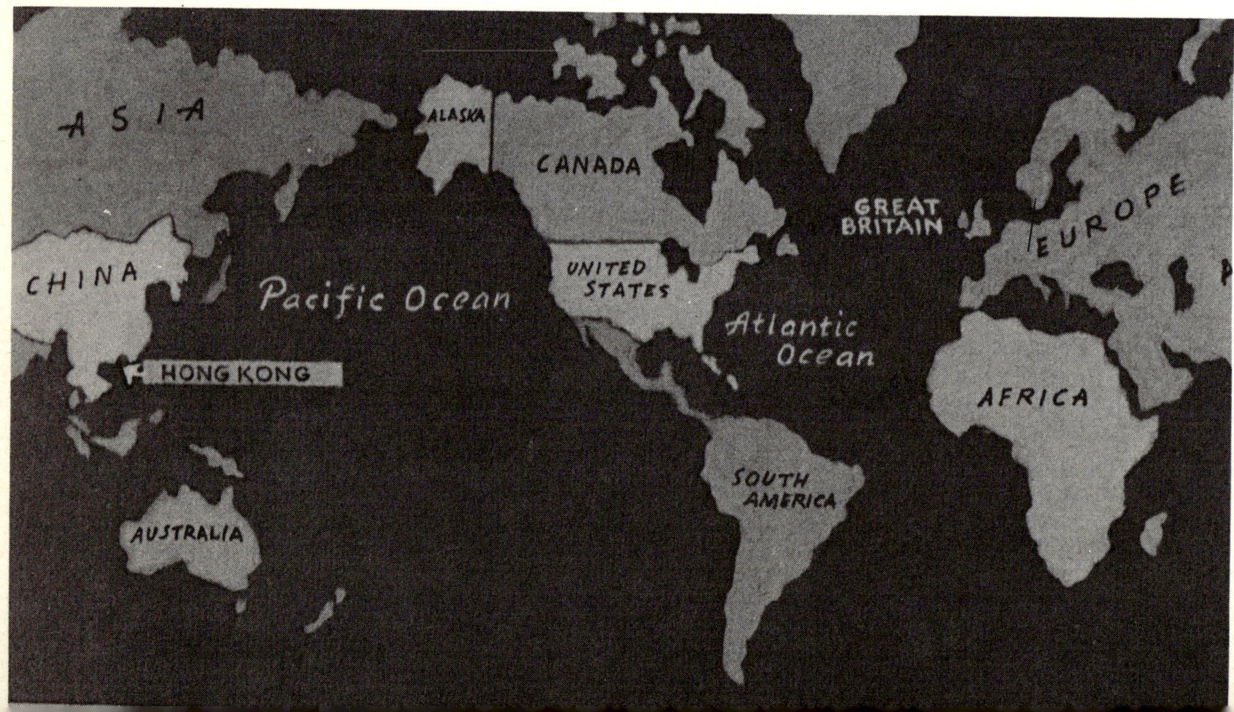

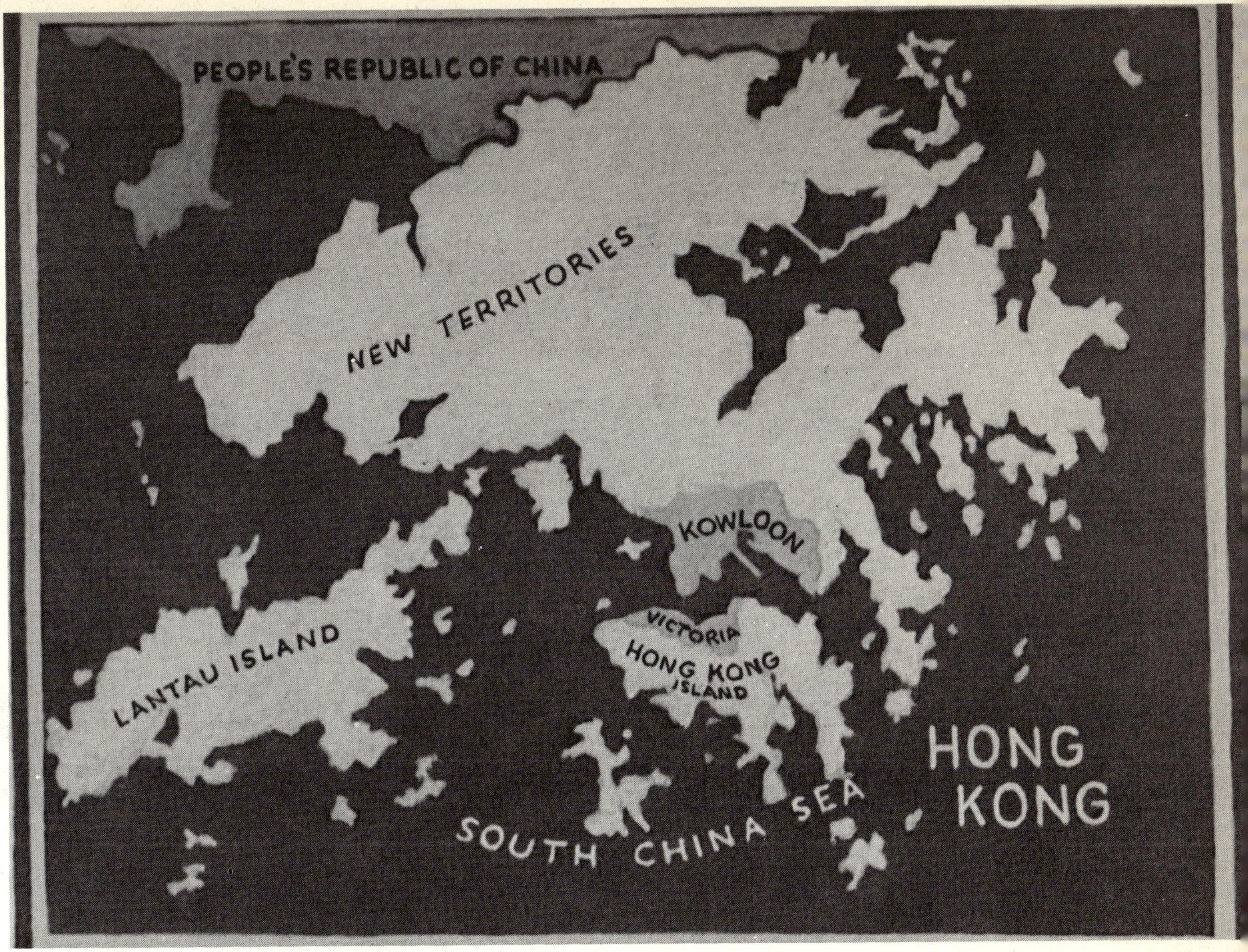

PEOPLE'S REPUBLIC OF CHINA
NEW TERRITORIES
KOWLOON
VICTORIA
HONG KONG ISLAND
LANTAU ISLAND
SOUTH CHINA SEA
HONG KONG

Part of Hong Kong is Britain's through a permanent treaty with China, signed in the mid 1800's. Other areas of the Colony were leased by China to Britain some years later. The lease expires in 1997. No one can say for sure if the lease will be renewed or if those leased areas of Hong Kong will revert to Chinese rule at that time.

There are well over four million people living in Hong Kong. Most of them are Chinese. It has been said of Hong Kong that there is too little space and too many people. This is a familiar cry in many parts of the world today.

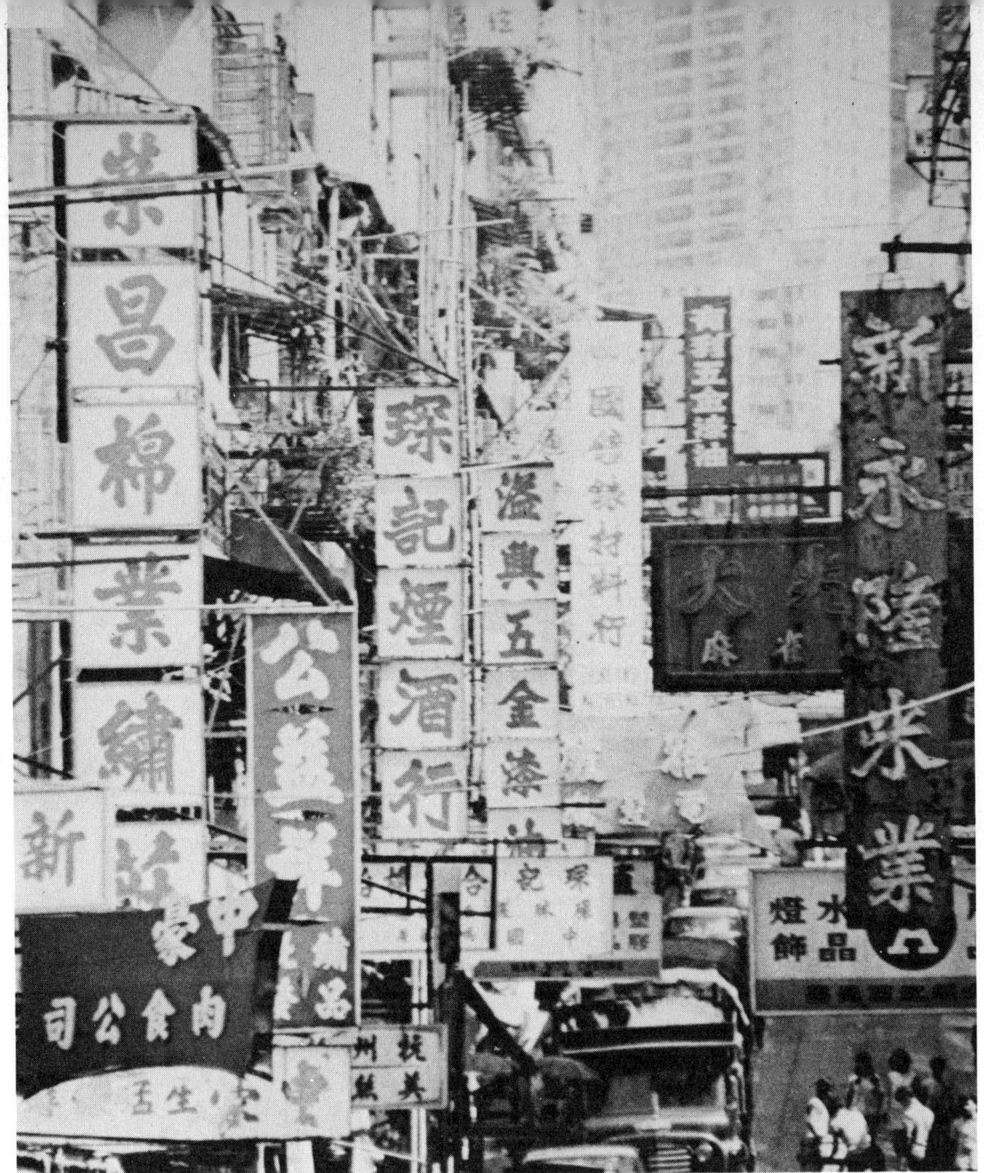

Crowded though it may be, Hong Kong sits like a jewel in the South China Sea. Her lights at night are more dazzling than a giant Fourth of July sparkler.

Hong Kong is a busy place at night. It is even busier by day and as dazzling. Gay multi-colored signs and banners splashed with Chinese characters attract the eye. Many bear legends in English as well.

Sidewalks bulge with people going about their daily lives. And thousands of tourists come and go, bent on seeing the sights of Hong Kong. Shops are as jammed as a too-full bean bag.

Rickshaws, the taxis of old which are pulled by jogging Chinese men, are fast disappearing from the streets of Hong Kong. These big-wheeled carriages with room for only one or two passengers are now mostly tourist attractions. Buses, modern-day taxis, and private cars have taken their place.

On some streets the clang of streetcars now mixes with the tinkle of temple bells. Honking automobile horns and the cries of hawkers peddling their wares add to the many sounds of Hong Kong.

New ways of doing things, new ways of living are having an effect on many young lives. Once, for example, few children of Hong Kong went to school. Today school is a must, and nearly all children of suitable age are in school.

The *water people*, the *boat people* of Hong Kong, are among those most greatly affected by the strong winds of change in today's world. By tradition they have been boat-dwellers, living on big junks and smaller boats called sampans.

Thousands of these people of the sea are found clustered in fishing villages along the waters surrounding various areas of Hong Kong. A boy named Li Po is one of them.

Until Li Po was nine years old he had never once set foot on dry land. He had lived his whole life on his father's fishing junk where he was born. And, at nine, Li Po had never been to school. As is the ancient Chinese custom, Po puts his family name, Li, before his given name.

Now Po and his family have moved from their junk to live in a house on land. The junk is still a fishing vessel, a means of livelihood, but it is no longer the family home. The junk now has a motor and is no longer dependent only on broad sails and wind to move it over the water. This change has made possible bigger catches of fish. More fish bring in more money to help feed the many hungry mouths in the family.

For centuries the boat people were not allowed to live or work ashore. They were born, grew up, lived out their lives and died aboard their boats. They were very, very poor. Their boats were very, very crowded.

Dogs, cats, chickens, pigs, and ducks were often part of family life afloat. The animals, along with the babies, learned to walk about the boats without falling overboard. However, accidents did sometimes happen and a tearful baby, a squealing pig, or a squalling cat had to be fished from the water.

The day-to-day activities of family life were carried on aboard the boats. Mothers or grandmothers prepared meals, washed clothes, and helped the men with fishing. Older children looked after younger ones and helped with other tasks as well.

Now, as they can, more and more of the water people are moving into homes ashore. They are encouraged by the government to do so. And children of the boat people, as well as those of the land, now go to school. Li Po and his brothers and sisters are among them. They are learning many things about the world in which they live and the amazing ways of life on land.

The Chinese language is made up of a number of different dialects. Cantonese is the main one spoken in Hong Kong. Teaching in Li Po's school is done in this dialect. English is taught as a second language.

Po's grandmother takes care of his younger brother and sister while his father and mother are away all day fishing. His grandfather now stays ashore most of the time. But sometimes he goes out to fish when the ache in his old bones is not too bad.

Living on land seems especially strange to Po's grandmother. All her long life she had been used only to the rolling pitch of the junk as it skimmed over the water or bobbed at anchor in the harbor. At first she felt "land sick" upon moving from the boat. She still feels awkward walking on solid ground. Po, however, already walks and runs with ease on rigid floors and pavements. He has learned to play tag and other such land games.

A long red ribbon hangs across the center beam of the Li's new, sparsely furnished house. Dangling from either end of the ribbon hang small bags of rice, sugar, beans, and money. Twigs of evergreen adorn the little bags. These tokens are appeals to the gods for good luck in this new home, this new way of life. The small offerings represent a great sacrifice on the part of the Li family, for the contents of the little bags are never too plentiful at the best of times.

To Li Po, running water and electricity seem a sort of magic. Each time water flows from the tap or a light comes on at the flip of a switch, he is a little surprised. But the very greatest marvel of all is the magic of pictures on the television set in Po's school.

When there is time, Po helps his father and grandfather mend their fishing nets. And he still goes out with his father on the junk to learn the ways of a fisherman. Mr. Li is a skilled junkmaster. He guides the junk along, threading his way through the busy traffic of Hong Kong's Victoria Harbor.

This beautiful waterway was once a place where pirates plied their wicked trade. Today Hong Kong is a great world trade center and the harbor is crowded with big cargo ships and passenger liners as well as junks, sampans, and *walla wallas.* Walla wallas are the water taxis of Hong Kong. They are so called because the first sampans to be used for that purpose were operated by an American whose home town was Walla Walla, Washington.

If the air becomes heavy and dark clouds appear, from time to time Po's father listens to his little radio. For with the approach of a typhoon, warnings are sent crackling over the air waves and storm flags are hoisted. Mr. Li, with the masters of other such craft, heeds the warnings and heads back to the safety of a typhoon shelter to wait out the storm. Po has known these storms all his life. He is always glad when they have the junk tied down and made secure against the fury of the typhoon.

Someday Po may spend time at sea-school in a special boat to learn ways of fishing other than those his father uses. He will be taught more about navigation and seamanship in a fishing vessel called a trawler. And he will learn better ways of caring for and marketing his catch.

Though many families like the Lis are land-based now, and some even have jobs on land, they are still water people. They still visit temples of the Sea Goddess, their special deity. She is *Tin Hau*, Heavenly Queen.

Tin Hau's birthday is the favorite festival of the water people. It falls on the twenty-third day of the third moon. The Chinese calendar is different from that used by the Western world. It is the lunar, or moon, calendar. The Chinese New Year, for example, does not start on January first. It begins on the first day of the first moon. This may fall in late January or sometime in February, according to our calendar.

Li Po shivers with excitement at the mere thought of sailing to the Tin Hau temple at Fat Tong Mun in Joss House Bay. He has been there many times throughout the year, but Tin Hau's birthday party is a gay time of special treats.

Bright pennants and birthday greetings to the Sea Goddess decorate the hundreds of boats that crowd the Bay. The music of flutes, the sound of gongs and the clashing of cymbals fills the air.

The tempting smell of food rises from the boats as special offerings of roast pig and chickens are prepared as birthday gifts for the Heavenly Queen. This is the boat people's way of saying thank you to Tin Hau. They are grateful to her for having kept them from harm during the typhoon season.

Though Li Po's life has changed, he is still very much one of the water people of Hong Kong, looking to Tin Hau for safe-keeping in rough seas.

A typical boat people's temple

Life has also changed for Wong Pei, a child of the land. Until she was eight years old Pei had never been beyond the small village in the People's Republic of China where she was born. But she had already attended the village school.

In addition to regular school subjects, Pei had to learn many mottoes written by the Republic's leader. And lectures about how one should conduct one's life were part of the daily routine.

Arithmetic came easy for Pei. Learning to read and write some of the thousands of characters used in Chinese writing came harder. Pei also worked in the fields outside the village where her mother and father worked all day.

Now Wong Pei and her family have left their village in the People's Republic. They live in a new factory town in Hong Kong, one of many built by the Hong Kong government. These towns offer shelter and a place to work to the tens of thousands of refugees who, like Pei's family, have fled mainland China to seek a different and freer way of life.

Pei's mother and father now work in one of the factories near their new home. Often the family has a happy time visiting with relatives who had come earlier to Hong Kong.

Pei and some of her brothers and sisters go to school atop the big building where they live. There are many such high-rise, low-rent buildings in the new towns, each with its own school.

Schools are crowded and, like some children in America, students go to school in shifts. Some go in the morning, others in the afternoon, while some attend evening classes.

Pei is in school from eight in the morning until one o'clock. After school she does her homework and helps her grandmother look after the younger children. Sometimes they play in the playground beside their building where there are slides and swings and things on which to climb.

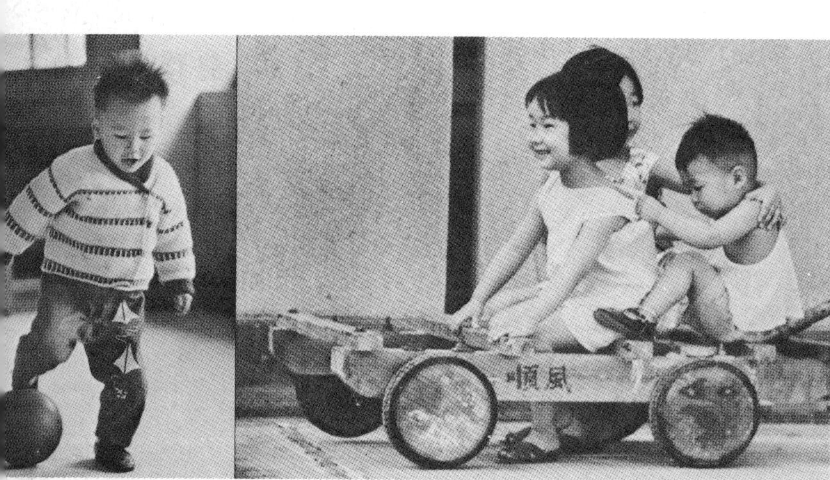

Pei also carefully tends the little garden growing in a box on the balcony outside the family flat on the fourth floor of the building.

Pei often hangs out the family wash. Bamboo poles extending out from the building serve as clotheslines. Poles and balcony railings are space-savers and most such buildings have an array of poles. The buildings are made colorful with bright clothing flapping in the breeze like so many flags.

Sometimes Pei misses the quiet and the open spaces of the fields and orchards of her native village where only a few hundred people live. She thinks often of the grandparents left behind. She is glad that one of her grandmothers came to Hong Kong with the family. Elders are given great respect in Chinese homes and attention is paid to the wisdom of their years.

Pei never tires of the many wonders of life in the big resettlement estate. And at mealtime when her rice bowl is fuller than it ever was in the village, she's especially happy to be in Hong Kong. Bits of chicken, fish, or pork are more plentiful on the family table now than ever before.

Gods are not allowed in the People's Republic so there were none in the Wongs' village home. But Grandmother remembers well the old ways before they were forbidden. Happily, she has placed a Kitchen God, *Tsao Wang*, in the new home. He is of paper and hangs near the stove. Grandmother has told the children that he keeps an eye on everything they do, especially anything naughty.

TSAO WANG

At the end of the year the god will be burned so that he can fly up to see the Great Heavenly Jade Emperor. There the Kitchen God will report on the family's deeds throughout the year. No one takes this very seriously, but now and then the children look the god's way to see if he is watching them.

Gradually Wong Pei is becoming used to the great flow of traffic in the street below her building. The automobiles of many colors are a never-ending source of wonder to her. Never before had she seen anything like them or the great trucks which haul gasoline and other supplies. Never had she seen the likes of the big buses jammed with passengers.

Pei had been used to seeing only carts pulled by bullocks, or by men and women. And never had Pei seen so many bicycles as in Hong Kong, There were few in her village who could afford such a luxury as a bicycle.

Unlike Pei, Sarah Jordan had been used to traffic all her life. She had always been used to big buses and automobiles and crowds of people. Sarah is an English girl, born in England. At ten, she had been going to school in her native London for several years. Most of the subjects she studied were similar to those studied by children her age in the United States and Canada. Sarah's father worked in an office in London not far from Buckingham Palace.

Sarah, too, now lives in Hong Kong. There her father works in a government office in the city of Victoria on Hong Kong Island, second largest of the Colony's many islands. Victoria, the seat of Hong Kong's government, is a blend of western culture and that of the East. The Colony's emblem displays the British Lion and the Chinese Dragon side by side. It is a symbol of a "live-and-let-live" understanding between the British and the Chinese people of Hong Kong.

Sarah lives in a flat in one of the modern high-rise buildings that are creeping up the hillsides of Hong Kong Island. They pierce the sky on the steep slopes of Victoria where land is very scarce. There are few private houses there or anywhere in the Colony.

In Hong Kong Sarah goes to a school much like the one she attended in England. Most of the students are British. But Chinese children and children of other origins go there too. Teaching is in English, with Chinese taught as a second language.

Hong Kong is a new and exciting world to Sarah. At first she was homesick for England and her friends there. But now she has begun to understand a little of the ways of the Chinese and to make friends with them.

boats
aeroplanes

Sometimes Sarah and her mother do their shopping in Victoria stores that are so British they seem like shops back in London. They also enjoy the Chinese shops on the Island and those across the harbor on the Kowloon Peninsula.

The city of Kowloon, on the Peninsula, is even more crowded than Victoria and is very Chinese. The two cities face each other across the water like happy neighbors, pleased with themselves and with each other.

Sometimes Sarah and her mother drive through the great tunnel beneath the water that links the two cities. And sometimes, more to Sarah's liking, they cross the harbor on one of the crowded ferries that take only foot passengers. The seven-minute trip costs twenty-five Hong Kong cents. That is about five cents in United States money. Those who ride on a lower deck may do so for about two cents American.

Sarah has learned that in Hong Kong the Buddhist and Tao religions have the most followers. There are also Chinese who, like Sarah's people, follow the Christian religion. And there are those who have yet other beliefs.

Sometimes strange things form a link in Sarah's mind between some of the Chinese people and people elsewhere. Troublesome ghosts were said to be disturbing some of the Chinese people working in a new building. This made Sarah think of the stories she had heard of ghosts and demons that haunt certain places in England. She had also heard of such things being a torment to people in the United States and many other places of the world as well.

Sarah learned that Buddhist priests were called in to get rid of the Hong Kong ghosts. The priests, dressed in yellow robes, went through each room of the tall building chanting prayers. They sprinkled water that had been blessed and incense ashes in all the dark corners.

There was also the beating of drums and the clanging of gongs to help scare the ghosts away. Afterward the people went back to work and Sarah was told that the ghosts hadn't bothered them again. The Chinese use noise made by drums, gongs, and exploding firecrackers to drive away all sorts of evil spirts.

When the government put on a drive to "Keep Hong Kong Clean," Sarah was especially busy. She joined with other children in keeping an eye out for litterbugs. All the children were very careful not to be litterbugs themselves. *Lap Sap Chung*, which is Cantonese for litterbug, was the enemy. And the people of Hong Kong were out to destroy him.

Sarah's father and the father of her friend, Jade Wu, work in the same office. Both men helped in making plans for the big cleanup of Hong Kong.

Jade has a pen pal, Pat, in far off Spokane, in the United States. They exchange letters in English which help Jade's knowledge of the language. Jade wrote to Pat about Lap Sap Chung and enclosed a picture of him. Pat then wrote Jade about Spokane's litter rally and its "Trash Eater." "Trash Eater" was a big steel goat who gulped down trash and said, "Please feed me, I'm hungry."

Jade and Sarah Jordan go to the same school. Jade, who was born in Hong Kong, also lives in a modern high-rise building. There is a Kitchen God in the Wu home and Door Gods hang on either side of the front door to keep evil spirits from entering.

The Chinese often enjoy symbols of the holidays of other cultures as well as those of their own. Santa Claus, for example, is cheerfully accepted by them. But they do not think of Christmas as a religious festival.

Lap Sap Chung

Jade enjoys the Western-type decorations that festoon downtown Kowloon and Victoria at Christmastime. But her favorite time of year is the Chinese New Year. Then there are big family dinner parties with glazed duck, melon soup, and other good things to eat. There are numerous private ceremonies and public affairs to attend. Jade always looks forward to the great Dragon Parade and the beautiful nightime flower market which are very special events of the New Year.

Jade's father is a university graduate and he once spent some time in the United States. Jade sometimes goes to concerts of Western music with her parents. And sometimes they attend the Chinese opera.

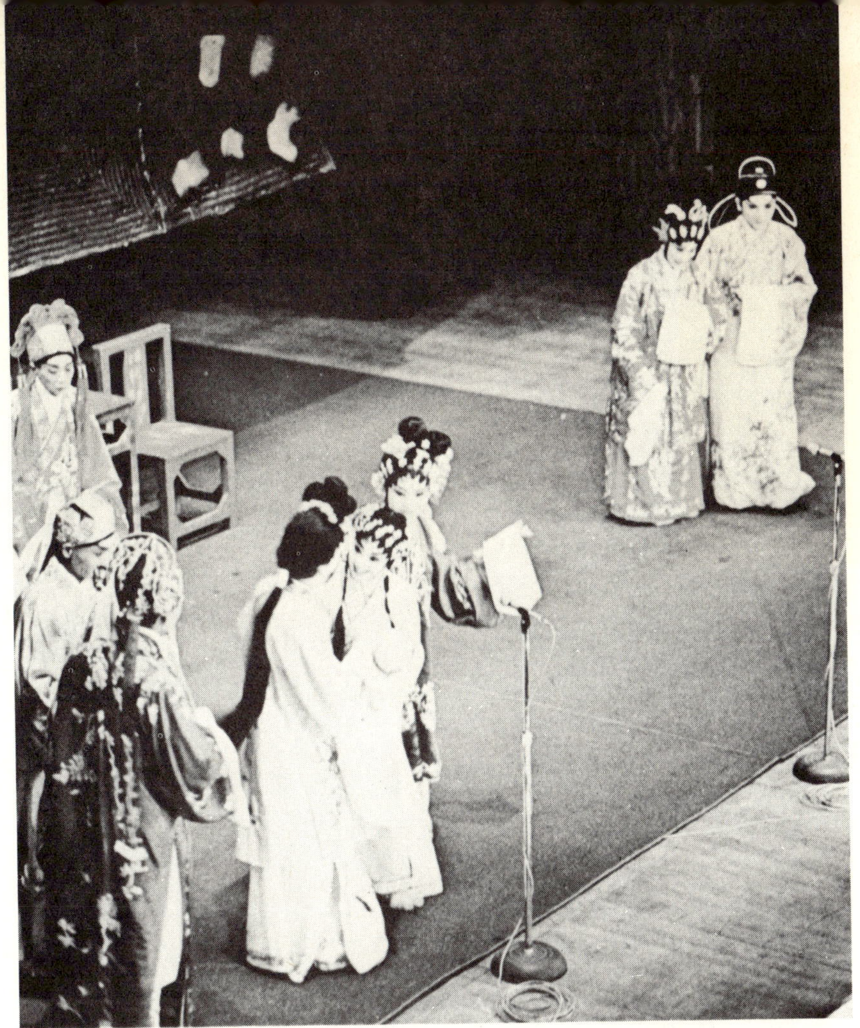

*Training in the perform-
ing arts starts young.*

Jade is studying music in school and has been playing the piano since she was in the first grade. She is learning to play the guitar too, and she likes rock and roll as well as classical music.

Jade has a bird for a pet. She keeps it in a bamboo cage. Her brother has a cricket which he keeps in a tiny cricket cage. Sometimes they take their pets, safe in their cages, for a walk in a nearby park to give them an airing.

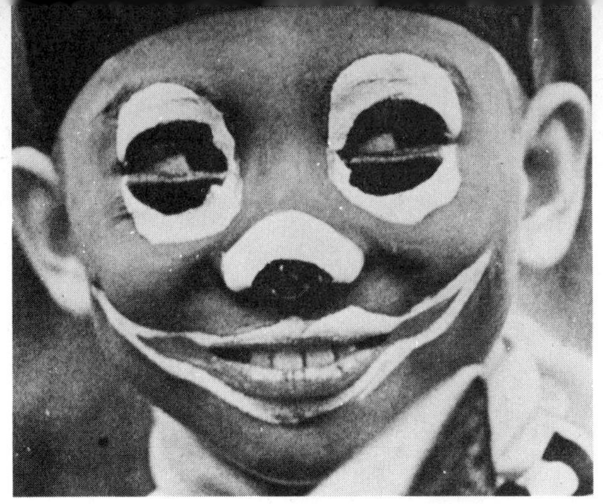

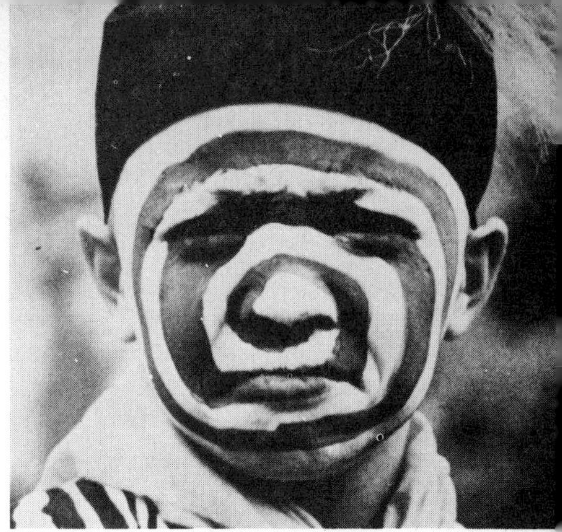

Peter Ling, like Jade, was born in Hong Kong and has lived there all his life. He is eleven. Peter's "milk" name, given to baby boys when they are a month old, is Chen. He has enjoyed school since the day he started when he was seven. It was then that he was given Peter as his "book" name.

Television is the great joy of Peter's life. He eagerly looks forward to the TV programs at his school. Once he took part in a program being filmed to be shown at all the Hong Kong schools. He would like to be a television cameraman or an actor when he grows up.

Peter's father has a small shop in Kowloon where he sells handbags, slippers, shirts, and other such things. He commutes to work by bus from the Ling home which is in an outlying district. Because he deals with so many tourists, Mr. Ling has adopted the Western custom of putting the family name last.

Mr. Ling keeps his shop open every day in the week. On Sundays, which have no religious meaning to the Lings, the family goes with him to the shop to spend the day. At noon, as a special treat, Mr. Ling takes them all to a teahouse to *yum cha.* Yum cha is Cantonese for "drink tea."

In the evening some teahouses become night clubs.

In olden days yum cha was a sort of tea break, a time just for drinking tea. Today yum cha means eating *dim sum* for breakfast or lunch as well as drinking tea. Dim sum means "small food."

The teahouse, or restaurant, where the Lings go is usually crowded with Chinese; tourists are seldom seen there. Sometimes they have to wait for a table. After they are seated, a big pot of tea is brought to the table first. Some is poured into each person's small bowl-like cup.

Then women with food on small carts or on trays suspended from their necks move among the tables for people to make their choices. It is a little like a cafeteria in reverse. Each woman offers a different kind of food. Mr. Ling orders, in turn, several kinds of dim sum.

Peter especially likes cooked chicken's feet and a little pastry of steamed rice filled with bits of shrimp. The steaming food is placed on the table in small round bamboo boxes. The size of the boxes varies according to the kinds of food. The amount of the bill is figured by the number and size of the boxes on the table.

As each box is chosen, Mr. Ling serves the family, lifting a portion from the box onto each small plate. Then everyone clicks away with his chopsticks, expertly using them to lift the food into his mouth.

Sometimes after lunch, if Mr. Ling's shop is crowded with tourists, Peter comes out from the small back room to help wait on customers. He feels quite pleased when English-speaking people can understand his halting school-boy English.

Sometimes Mr. Ling sends Peter to guide tourists through the hustle and bustle of crowded streets to their hotels. Or he may take them to another shop they have asked about.

Peter guides the visitors through wide streets and narrow where the sidewalks are so crowded people have to push their way through.

He takes them up steep little alley-like side streets with their gay signs and decorations. These streets are not much more than a set of broad steps leading up the steep hillsides from one level to another. Tiny shops line these ladder-like streets where no vehicles can get through.

Street vendors cry their wares, which may be anything from bead trinkets to baby straps. The baby straps are used to keep little ones securely tied to the backs of those caring for them. Mothers, grandmothers, and even very small girls are to be seen with babies strapped on behind.

Peter is usually offered a tip, or "tea money," for his services. But he refuses the money, for his father has taught him not to accept such tips. There are those who beg for money, but not the Lings. It is enough, Mr. Ling feels, to know that one has been helpful.

Ding Chau is about Peter's age. He is a country boy, one of the farming people who live in the rural valleys and rolling hills of the New Territories area of Hong Kong. Here small rice paddies and tiny garden plots have been handed down from generation to generation.

Here water buffalo are used as work horses. They pull the plows that till the land. Farmers carry water in buckets that hang from either end of a bamboo pole carried across their shoulders. But now, gradually, small mechanical farm equipment and better methods of irrigation are being put into use.

Duck, chicken, and pig farms, as well as the small houses of little villages, dot the New Territories landscape. Ding Chau lives on one of the duck farms near the border that separates Hong Kong from the Chinese province of Kwangtung. His people have lived there for generations raising ducks. How long no one knows, but it is certain that they settled there hundreds of years ago while the region was still part of ancient China. It has been only since 1898 that this land was leased to the British for ninety-nine years and called the New Territories as part of extended Hong Kong.

Chau's father sells ducks and duck eggs in the nearby markets and to restaurants in Kowloon. Chau gathers eggs and helps feed the ducks.

Chau has never been to the city, but he goes to the new village school, among the first in his family to do so. Nearly everyone in Chau's village is related to everyone else, all belonging to the same clan. Chau is getting on well in learning to read. He eagerly waits for the mobile library which brings books to his village.

Chau likes to draw and to paint pictures. One of his pictures was chosen to hang in an exhibit of children's artwork. The exhibit was held in the art gallery in the City Hall in downtown Victoria. Chau hopes that one of his paintings will be chosen for the next such exhibit. If it is, perhaps then he will be able to go on the bus all the twenty miles into Kowloon, then take the ferry across to the Island to see his painting hanging with the others there in the City Hall.

The Chinese follow a twelve-year cycle of years. Animal names tell the sequence. There is the Year of the Rat, the Year of the Ox, the Tiger, and the Rabbit. Then comes the Year of the Dragon, the Snake, and the Horse. These are followed by the Year of the Ram, the Monkey, Rooster, Dog, and the Year of the Pig. At the end of the twelve years, the cycle repeats.

Ding Chau is a Year of the Dragon boy. This pleases him very much. The dragon is said to bring rain which is good for the crops—and good for helping to fill up the duck ponds.

Ding Chau and the other children told about in this book, and the many boys and girls of the land, the water, and the city whose pictures appear here, represent some of the many faces of Hong Kong. They have a different life style and speak a different tongue than most children of the Western world. But they have a common bond with children everywhere. For they, as children the world over, share the language of laughter and tears, of joy and sadness, of hopes and dreams.

Li Po, Wong Pei, and the others are all children of Hong Kong. They are among our neighbors throughout the world, neighbors of the far-off East.

INDEX

Children in the changing world of modern Hong Kong is the theme of this unusual book, written from first-hand observation by Terry Shannon and illustrated with dozens of arresting and meaningful photographs, many of them taken "on location" during the author's stay in that fascinating spot. Today almost half of Hong Kong's teeming population of well over four million are boys and girls under the age of sixteen, most of them Chinese. For almost all of them life is very different from that of their parents growing up in the Hong Kong of only a generation ago. Miss Shannon takes a penetrating look at a variety of their life styles — for example, what it is like to be children of the "boat people" who, until recent times, were born to live out their entire lives on junks and sampans in Hong Kong Harbor, but who now occupy modern dwellings on shore and go to modern schools where TV is a teaching tool and English is taught as a second language.

Using as her prototypes a number of boys and girls of different social and economic backgrounds, the author skillfully contrasts the old ways with the new to give young American readers a picture of childhood in a far-off land, but making it so real and contemporary that it might well seem a part of their own experience.

TERRY SHANNON'S career as a writer has taken her to many unusual spots on the face of the globe — from under the sea in a submersible to a mountain peak in Switzerland. An enthusiastic traveler, she is equally at home in Hong Kong and Paris, or in a remote Eskimo village in the northernmost part of Alaska. Research for her many books (most of them done in collaboration with her working partner, illustrator Charles Payzant) has provided her with special knowledge of such diverse subjects as U. S. underseas exploration, icebreaking in Arctic waters, and the saving of endangered species in zoos throughout the world. A native of Bellingham, Washington, Miss Shannon now lives in the Southern California seaside community of Corona del Mar. Her many successful titles for young people include *Windows In The Sea, New At The Zoo, Ride The Ice Down!,* and *Smokejumpers And Fire Divers.*